RECLAIM
YOUR
ROYAL
INHERITANCE

RECLAIM YOUR ROYAL INHERITANCE

Lessons from Fairytales, Faith, and
Courageously Navigating Spiritual Warfare

Dr. Veronica Deas

publish
your gift

RECLAIM YOUR ROYAL INHERITANCE

Copyright © 2025 Veronica Deas

All rights reserved.

Published by Publish Your Gift®
An imprint of Purposely Created Publishing Group, LLC

No part of this book may be reproduced, distributed, or transmitted in any form by any means, graphic, electronic, or mechanical, including photocopy, recording, taping, or by any information storage or retrieval system, without permission in writing from the publisher, except in the case of reprints in the context of reviews, quotes, or references.

Scripture quotations are taken from the Holy Bible, unless otherwise noted.

Printed in the United States of America

ISBN: 978-1-64484-666-7 (print)
ISBN: 978-1-64484-667-4 (ebook)

Special discounts are available on bulk quantity purchases by book clubs, associations, and special interest groups. For details email vedeas@gmail.com.

TABLE OF CONTENTS

Introduction 1

Chapter 1: Take the Blinders Off and Claim Your Inheritance 3

Chapter 2: The Chosen Path 13

Chapter 3: The Biggest Spiritual Warfare Hidden in a Fairytale 21

Chapter 4: Who Are You? 31

Chapter 5: What Do You Have? 39

Chapter 6: Hot Air 47

Conclusion 55

About the Author 57

INTRODUCTION

The enemy of our destiny often hides in plain sight. Sometimes it takes a fairy tale princess, a dedicated teacher, and a girl in ruby slippers to help us see the truth about spiritual warfare and our divine inheritance. For me, this revelation came through three beloved movies: *Cinderella*, *To Sir, With Love*, and *The Wizard of Oz*. What began as simple entertainment became powerful lenses through which God would teach me about identity, purpose, and claiming my spiritual inheritance.

I adored *Cinderella* because her journey went beyond mere fairy tale romance. I delighted in *To Sir, With Love* because of Sidney Poitier's life-changing role as a teacher who dealt with the challenges of London's toughest school. His character showed strength, inspiring a generation to see their natural potential. Lastly, I was drawn to *The Wizard of Oz* and Dorothy's deep inner journey of finding herself.

Each movie showed a detailed form of spiritual warfare—the inner and outer battles we face against forces that challenge our growth and identity. In *Cinderella*, her family's harsh patterns took away her inheritance, but her journey of self-worth finally allowed her to get back not just her prince, but her dignity and purpose.

In *To Sir, With Love*, the spiritual battle was about making hard choices. People often pick the easy way, but God has made a special path for each of us. This path might not be easy at first, but what you gain from following it is worth much more than any hard times you face.

The Wizard of Oz looked at spiritual warfare on an even deeper level—fighting inner limits, society's expectations, and the voices that try to lower one's sense of destiny. Dorothy's adventure was less about an outer Yellow Brick Road and more about her inner journey to understanding herself.

As I grew up, these movies changed from simple entertainment into deep spiritual stories. They showed layers of meaning about personal growth, identity, and the human spirit's amazing strength.

Now, let me share my journey of how God opened my eyes to see the inheritance He had waiting for me all along.

CHAPTER 1

TAKE THE BLINDERS OFF AND CLAIM YOUR INHERITANCE

Different Yet Never Alone

As a child, I was different—a bit of a loner, yet never truly alone. I had wonderful siblings who filled my days with laughter. When they were up to no good, I would laugh along, and when they were caught, we would all share in the punishment. We never told on each other, and those were truly great times.

Dolls, Dreams, and Stories

I would play alone with my different dolls: the Julia doll (my Black Barbie), the actual Barbie doll (Caucasian Barbie), and paper dolls. I enjoyed changing their outfits, making up stories, and thinking about their lives. The Jackson 5, my favorite singing group, also sparked my thinking. I would dream of being part of their family, making up stories of a glamorous movie star life. With such creativity around me, I could have easily become a fashion designer, writer, or movie maker. I was always drawn to stories that ended with "and they lived happily ever after."

Cinderella's Hidden Battle

Cinderella's story reveals more than a fairy tale—it shows us a spiritual battle where a young woman had to first recognize her true worth before she could claim her royal birthright.

Cinderella's father married what we would today call a gold digger. When he died, he left Cinderella his inheritance. However, her stepmother and stepsisters quickly stole this inheritance. They were sent by the enemy to steal her wealth, kill her dreams, and destroy her destiny.

Eyes Opened to Identity

A prince entered her life and took the blinders from her eyes. Once she saw her natural worth and identity, she began to fight back and finally got back everything that had been stolen from her. Without knowing it, this prince was closely tied to her destiny.

I was reminded that the Bible says, "The thief cometh not, but for to steal, and to kill, and to destroy: I am come that they might have life, and that they might have it more abundantly." (John 10:10). Those who believe in God are given back their inheritance. His Word states that Jesus Christ came to give us life and life more abundantly.

Helpers or Destroyers of Destiny

I learned from Cinderella's story a key life lesson: people will either help you reach your destiny or try to destroy it. The key lies in good judgment—understanding who has been sent into your life and for what purpose. Are they helpers of destiny or destroyers of destiny?

Good judgment is very important. It guides us in making life's key choices. If you find yourself feeling empty or lacking peace, look at the people closest to you—they might be causing your problems.

Blinded by Familiar Places

Cinderella's story shows how places we live can blind us. Her father failed to see that his new wife was a "destiny thief." Despite his wealth and Cinderella being his rightful heir, her stepmother for a time robbed her of her inheritance. Only when Cinderella's eyes were opened did she get back what was hers.

People must remove their blinders to follow the path God has written (Psalm 139:16). Once you can see clearly, don't let outside forces beat you. Learn to take back your destiny.

Claiming My Own Inheritance

My life changed when I accepted Jesus Christ as my Lord and Savior. I began studying God's Word to understand my true identity. The Scripture is like a godly will, showing the inheritance promised to every believer. Salvation is not just about the afterlife, but about getting freedom, wealth, safety, and victory here on Earth.

As Ephesians 1:11 states: "In whom also we have obtained an inheritance, being predestinated according to the purpose of Him who worketh all things after the counsel of His own will."

I found out that I am special, a chosen vessel. Being royal is my share. As part of a chosen group, I have a clear right to my inheritance.

As 1 Peter 2:9 declares: "But ye are a chosen generation, a royal priesthood, an holy nation, a peculiar people; that ye should shew forth the praises of Him who hath called you out of darkness into His marvelous light."

And as Romans 8:17 proclaims: "Now if we are children, then we are heirs—heirs of God and co-heirs with Christ, if indeed we share in His sufferings in order that we may also share in His glory."

The Greater Purpose Revealed

Just as Cinderella had to recognize her true worth before claiming her inheritance, I too would discover that removing spiritual blinders was only the beginning. My journey, like the paths of many others, would take unexpected turns, each one designed to reveal God's greater purpose.

Key Spiritual Lessons

Cinderella teaches us:

1. People are either *helpers of destiny* or *destroyers of destiny*—discern the difference.

2. Familiarity can blind us from seeing God's truth about our worth.

3. Our inheritance is already secured through Christ; spiritual blindness is what keeps us from claiming it.

4. Good judgment, rooted in God's Word, protects our destiny.

Biblical Foundations

Key Scriptures that anchor these lessons are:

- John 10:10 – "The thief comes only to steal, kill, and destroy; Christ came to give abundant life."

- Ephesians 1:11 – "In Him we have obtained an inheritance, predestined according to His purpose."

- 1 Peter 2:9 – "You are a chosen generation, a royal priesthood, called out of darkness into His light."

- Romans 8:17 – "We are heirs of God and co-heirs with Christ, sharing in His glory."

Reflect and Reclaim
Identity and Inheritance

Who in your life today is a *destiny helper* and who may be acting as a *destiny thief*? How can you discern the difference more clearly?

....

....

....

....

....

....

....

....

....

....

....

....

....

....

....

....

....

What "blinders" might be keeping you from seeing your true worth in Christ?

Ephesians 1:11 speaks about inheritance. What part of your inheritance in Christ do you feel you've been overlooking or not yet claiming?

How does familiarity with your environment or relationships influence your ability to see God's promises clearly?

CHAPTER 2

THE CHOSEN PATH

Childhood Lessons in Teaching

As I said in the last chapter, my teaching journey began early while playing with and "teaching" my dolls. In high school, I met Mrs. Stewart, a stylish accounting teacher who inspired me to study business. Her impact guided me to get a degree in business and later, a master of business administration (MBA). At the time, I thought accounting was my planned path.

When Plans Take a Detour

However, life rarely follows a straight line. An unexpected chance to teach came up, changing my work journey in a way that reminded me of the film *To Sir, With Love*. Sidney Poitier's character—first looking for work as an engineer—found himself pushed into teaching. While he thought teaching would be just a quick job, it ended up showing him what he was meant to do and brought out his best gifts.

Finding Purpose in an Unexpected Place

My own story was like this. Despite my first dreams of becoming a model—shaped by my childhood love of dressing dolls and my love for fashion—I found myself moving from accounting to teaching. This wasn't just a job change, but a spiritual journey of finding myself. Just as Poitier's character used his special wisdom to connect with and inspire students, I found my real purpose in teaching.

God's Hand in the Detours

While getting my Ed.D. in education and leadership, I saw that this path was planned by God. What seemed like an unexpected turn was, really, a carefully made route that would wake up my hidden potential and let me help with a higher purpose.

The wisdom in Proverbs 18:16 connects deeply: "A man's gift makes room for him, and brings him before great men." My journey proves this deep truth. The path chosen for me—not by my own plan, but by godly leading—made space for my true gifts to show up and grow.

Life Written Before We Begin

Psalm 139:14-16 further shows this idea of a planned-ahead purpose:

"I will praise You, for I am fearfully and wonderfully made;
Marvelous are Your works,
And that my soul knows very well.
My frame was not hidden from You,
When I was made in secret,
And skillfully wrought in the lowest parts of the earth.
Your eyes saw my substance, being yet unformed.
And in Your book they all were written,
The days fashioned for me,
When as yet there were none of them."

This passage reminds us that our lives are not random. God has a special plan for each of us; a design carefully made before our first breath. He sees far more than we can see and shapes our lives in ways that help us discover who we're meant to be and what we're meant to do.

Trust the Path God Made

Always remember: The path made for you is not about fitting what others expect, but about finding and using the special gifts placed in your spirit. Trust in the journey, for it is carefully made to bring your most real self into the light.

Like Sidney Poitier's character, what appears to be a detour may actually be divine redirection toward your true calling. When we surrender our plans to God's purpose, we discover that His path leads not only to our destiny but also prepares us for the battles we'll face in claiming it.

Key Spiritual Lessons

To Sir, With Love teaches us:

1. Detours often reveal our true calling more than our original plans.

2. God plants gifts in us early and uses life experiences to draw them out.

3. Every step, even the unexpected ones, is part of His divine blueprint.

4. Trusting God's path leads to purpose, peace, and alignment with destiny.

Biblical Foundations

Key Scriptures that anchor these lessons are:

- Proverbs 16:9 – "In their hearts humans plan their course, but the Lord establishes their steps."

- Proverbs 18:16 – "A man's gift makes room for him, and brings him before great men."

- Psalm 139:14-16 – "I am fearfully and wonderfully made … all the days ordained for me were written in your book before one of them came to be."

- Jeremiah 29:11 – "I know the plans I have for you, declares the Lord, plans to prosper you and not to harm you."

Reflect and Reclaim
Calling and Detours

Looking back, how have unexpected detours in your life revealed hidden gifts or purpose?

Where do you sense God is redirecting you right now, and how can you trust His plan over your own?

Proverbs 16:9 reminds us the Lord establishes our steps. How does this verse change the way you view past disappointments?

What gifts (Proverbs 18:16) do you sense God is making room for in this season of your life?

CHAPTER 3

THE BIGGEST SPIRITUAL WARFARE HIDDEN IN A FAIRY TALE

The Mind, the Blood, the Weapons, and Getting Ready for War

While understanding our identity and path is crucial, we must also learn to recognize and fight the spiritual battles that come with claiming our purpose. Once we've discovered our calling—as we explored through *To Sir, With Love*—we must prepare for the warfare that inevitably comes with walking in our divine assignment.

No story illustrates this better than *The Wizard of Oz*, where seemingly simple choices reveal profound spiritual truths about warfare and victory.

The Wizard of Oz is more than a simple fairy tale—it is a deep spiritual story showing key insights into spiritual warfare, personal change, and the journey to understanding one's godly identity and purpose. The Holy Spirit has revealed the hidden spiritual parts of this well-known story, asking us to look past what's on the surface.

Dorothy's First Struggle

Dorothy, whose name means "Gift of God," lived in a small town in Kansas City. Her mind was under attack by feelings of not being happy and being bored. She began dreaming of a different life, singing about a world "somewhere over the rainbow," thinking that life would be better somewhere else.

Her faithful friend, Toto, gave her stability during this hard time. When her neighbor threatened to take Toto away, Dorothy made a plan to run away to escape her current life.

The Life-Changing Storm

Suddenly, Dorothy went through a Euroclydon wind—a life-changing spiritual storm. As the winds raged, she hit her head, passed out, and was taken in her dreams to the land of Oz. The storm wasn't meant for harm; it was part of God's plan.

When her house fell from the sky, God used it to stop one of the evil rulers who controlled the eastern part of Oz. The ruby slippers—which held special power from God—were taken away from this defeated enemy.

Spiritual Power and Protection

When Dorothy stepped out of her house, she met the people of Oz and Glinda, a beautiful helper who was like the Holy Spirit. The Wicked Witch of the West came to try to take the power of the ruby slippers. But Glinda quickly put the shoes on Dorothy's feet, which kept her safe and protected.

The ruby slippers, like Cinderella's royal inheritance, represented Dorothy's God-given authority—something the enemy tried to steal but could never truly take away once she understood its power.

Friends and Spiritual Weapons

On her journey down the Yellow Brick Road, Dorothy was joined by three friends, each showing key spiritual weapons:

- The Scarecrow needed a brain - showing the importance of a sound, peaceful mind.
- The Tin Man needed a heart - showing love that pushes out fear.
- The Lion needed courage - showing spiritual power and lasting strength.

These friends mirror the promise in Scripture found in 2 Timothy 1:7: "God has not given us a spirit of fear, but of power, love, and a sound mind."

Fighting in Enemy Land

In the enemy's land, Dorothy faced many challenges. The Wicked Witch sent an army to catch her, trying to take away her power. However, the ruby slippers—representing the blood of Jesus—gave her supernatural protection. No matter what the enemy tried, nothing could hurt Dorothy.

Facing False Powers

The Wizard of the Emerald City at first seemed powerful, asking Dorothy to get the witch's broom as payment for him helping her return home. This showed the spiritual truth that sometimes what looks like an answer is really a distraction or a false path.

When Toto found out the Wizard was just a man behind a curtain—all show with no real power—it showed how useless it is to seek help from powerless sources.

The Final Truth

Glinda, representing the Holy Spirit, shared the deepest truth: Dorothy always had the power to return home. By clicking her heels three times—representing the Father, Son, and Holy Spirit—she could rise above her current situation.

Key Spiritual Lessons

The Wizard of Oz teaches us:

1. The enemy often attacks the mind first, sowing dissatisfaction and fear.

2. Spiritual battles are won through faith, not fear.

3. False sources of power will always be exposed; only God's Spirit leads to freedom.

4. The truth of our authority in Christ has been with us all along.

Biblical Foundations

Key Scriptures that anchor these lessons are:

- 2 Timothy 1:7 – "God has not given us a spirit of fear, but of power, love, and a sound mind."

- **Ephesians 6:10** – "Be strong in the LORD, and in the power of His might."

- **Colossians 2:14-15** – "Blotting out the handwriting of ordinances that was against us, which was contrary to us, and took it out of the way, nailing it to His cross; And having spoiled principalities and powers, He made a shew of them openly, triumphing over them in it."

- **Hebrews 13:5** – "He will never leave you nor forsake you."

Reflect and Reclaim
Warfare and Authority

How has the enemy attacked your *mind* with dissatisfaction or fear recently, and how can you combat it with truth?

What current "storm" in your life might actually be God's setup for breakthrough?

Which of the three weapons—a sound mind, love, or courage—do you need most right now, and why?

Where might you be depending on a "false source of power" (like the Wizard) instead of relying fully on God's Spirit?

CHAPTER 4

WHO ARE YOU?

Created in His Image

God made us to be like Him in two ways—in how we look and how we act. Think about it: God is a Spirit who creates and leads. To truly live like He meant us to, we need His Spirit in us. His Spirit guides us to create good things and take care of all He has made. When we speak and act, we should do it in ways that show we're His children. If we're not living this way, something has gone wrong.

The Purpose of Identity

As I learned more about who God made me to be, I remembered something Dr. Myles Munroe once said that really struck me: "If you do not know the purpose of a thing, abuse is inevitable." This truth helped me understand why knowing our identity in God is so important.

If we don't know what God made us for, we might waste the gifts He gave us. The enemy tries to trick us into giving up our power to lead our own lives, but Jesus has given us back our place as children who will share in God's kingdom.

Identity and Inheritance

Understanding who we are in God naturally leads us to discover what He's given us. Just as a loving father gives good gifts to his children, our heavenly Father has given us a covenant—His most powerful promise—that confirms and supports our identity in Him.

Key Spiritual Lessons

The lesson of identity, reinforced by Dr. Myles Munroe's wisdom teaches us:

1. Our true identity is rooted in being created in God's image.

2. Not knowing our identity leads to misuse or neglect of our gifts.

3. The enemy's goal is to distort identity, but Christ restores it.

4. Identity is inseparable from inheritance—knowing who we are reveals what we have.

Biblical Foundations

Key Scriptures that anchor these lessons are:

- Genesis 1:27 – "God created mankind in His own image."

- John 1:12 – "To all who received Him, He gave the right to become children of God."

- Romans 8:17 – "We are heirs of God and co-heirs with Christ."

- Ephesians 2:10 – "We are God's handiwork, created in Christ Jesus to do good works."

Reflect and Reclaim
Identity and Purpose

How do you define your identity right now, and how does it align with God's truth in Genesis 1:27?

Dr. Myles Munroe said, "If you do not know the purpose of a thing, abuse is inevitable." Where in your life have you seen this principle play out?

Which lies of the enemy about your identity are hardest for you to resist?

What promises from God (John 1:12, Romans 8:17) confirm your identity when you feel unsure of who you are?

CHAPTER 5

WHAT DO YOU HAVE?

God's Covenant Through Christ

Mankind has a covenant with God through Jesus Christ. As I stated earlier, Dorothy's mind was under attack. She thought a better world was somewhere over the rainbow, but she was *living* in the rainbow.

The Rainbow as God's Promise

The rainbow is God's sign of His covenant. His promise. Back in Noah's time, God sent a flood because of sin. But then God promised, using the rainbow as His sign, that He would never flood the whole Earth again. The rainbow means we're safe from the flood. You might think it's odd to compare being safe under the rainbow and looking over it. But sometimes we think life would be better somewhere else.

Safe and Loved at Home

Dorothy couldn't see how safe and loved she was at home. Many people dream about the future but miss the good things happening now. In the movie, the rainbow shows how God keeps us safe in hard times. When storms pass, they often lead us in new ways.

Storms That Protect

The storm didn't hurt Dorothy, instead, it stopped the evil witch. This shows how God can turn bad things into good things that help us.

God Uses Hardship for Growth

God can even use our mistakes and hardships to help us grow. Sometimes the most important lessons come through disappointment, as Dorothy discovered when she placed her hope in the wrong source. Her experience with the Wizard would teach her—and us—a crucial lesson about where to put our trust.

Key Spiritual Lessons

Dorothy's story teaches us:

1. God's covenant is unbreakable, symbolized by the rainbow.

2. We often overlook the blessings we already have by searching "somewhere else."

3. Storms can serve as divine protection, redirecting us toward God's plan.

4. Disappointments expose false sources of trust and point us back to God.

Biblical Foundations

Key Scriptures that anchor these lessons are:

- Genesis 9:13 – "I have set my rainbow in the clouds, and it will be the sign of the covenant between me and the earth."

- Romans 8:28 – "God works all things together for the good of those who love Him."

- Isaiah 41:10 – "Do not fear, for I am with you … I will strengthen you and help you."

Reflect and Reclaim
Covenant and Trust

How do you personally view God's covenant? Is it a distant idea, or a present reality in your life?

What blessings are you currently overlooking by thinking "life would be better somewhere else"?

Recall a storm or disappointment in your life that later redirected you toward something better. How did God use it?

Where are you most tempted to place your trust in "false sources," and how does God's covenant promise anchor you instead?

CHAPTER 6

HOT AIR

The Wizard's Empty Promises

After finding out the Wizard was fake, full of hot air, Dorothy was shocked and sad. She had hoped the Wizard would keep his promise and send her home.

The Balloon That Left

The Wizard offered to take Dorothy home in a hot air balloon, but the balloon left without her. Again, she felt hopeless, and she began to cry with her friends. They wanted the best for Dorothy.

Temporary People vs. True Support

It's good to have people around you who will cheer for you, not just put up with you. People who are around just to get what they need are like that hot air balloon. They stay with you when they need you, but when they don't need you anymore, they will leave you like the Wizard did.

God's Faithfulness in Every Season

But there is One who never leaves. Unlike those who come and go like hot air balloons, God promises, "I will never leave you nor forsake you." This truth reminds us that while people may disappoint us, God remains faithful through every season of our journey.

Bringing It All Together

As we've seen through these three powerful stories, God uses different seasons and experiences to reveal our true identity, purpose, and authority in Him. Now let's bring these truths together to understand how we can fully walk in all that God has for us.

Key Spiritual Lessons

Together, the three timeless stories, anchored in Scripture, teach us:

1. Like *Cinderella,* we must discern between destiny helpers and those who come with empty promises.

2. Like the teacher in *To Sir, With Love,* we discover purpose by walking faithfully in the path God sets before us, even when people fail us.

3. Like Dorothy, we learn that storms and disappointments reveal where true authority and protection come from—Christ alone.

4. All three remind us that identity, inheritance, and victory are secure in God's presence, not in the shifting loyalty of people.

Biblical Foundations

Key Scriptures that anchor these lessons are:

- Matthew 7:15-16 – "Watch out for false prophets. They come to you in sheep's clothing, but inwardly they are ferocious wolves. By their fruit you will recognize them …."

- Galatians 6:9 – "Let us not become weary in doing good, for at the proper time we will reap a harvest if we do not give up."

- Psalm 46:1 – "God is our refuge and strength, an ever-present help in trouble."

- Jeremiah 17:7 – "But blessed is the one who trusts in the Lord, whose confidence is in Him."

- Hebrews 13:5 – "… For He Himself has said, 'I will never leave you nor forsake you.'"

Reflect and Reclaim
God's Faithfulness vs. Empty Promises

Who in your life may be like the "hot air balloon"—present only when they need something from you? How can you set healthier boundaries?

How do you typically respond when people disappoint you? How could you shift that response to lean more on God's faithfulness?

In what ways has God proven His promise to "never leave you nor forsake you" (Hebrews 13:5) in your past?

How do the combined lessons from *Cinderella*, *To Sir, With Love*, and *The Wizard of Oz* strengthen your confidence in God's presence and plan for your life?

CONCLUSION

Only through the Son can you access the Father and the Holy Spirit to fulfill your destiny and have everlasting life.

John 3:16 says, "For God so loved the world, that He gave His only begotten Son, that whosoever believeth in Him should not perish, but have everlasting life."

Spiritual warfare has been going on since people first went wrong in the book of Genesis. The enemy, by tricking them, stole Adam and Eve's gift from God. God gave Adam a choice.

As Genesis 2:16-17 says, "Of every tree of the garden you may freely eat; but of the tree of the knowledge of good and evil you shall not eat, for in the day that you eat of it you shall surely die."

Life presents us with countless choices, each one shaping our destiny. As Jeremiah 1:5 reminds us, "Before I formed you in the womb I knew you," suggesting a divine blueprint for our lives. By aligning our choices with God's divine plan, we can fulfill our purpose on Earth.

Psalm 139:16 says, "Your eyes saw my substance, being yet unformed. And in Your book, they all were written, the days fashioned for me, When as yet there were none of them."

As we journey through life, let us remember the timeless wisdom found within Scripture and the films we've explored. By recognizing the spiritual battles that surround us and tapping into the power of God's Word, we can overcome adversity, fulfill our divine purpose, and experience the victory Christ offers.

Looking back at these three stories, I see how God used them to shape my understanding. *Cinderella* helped me understand how to claim what God had already given me, *To Sir, With Love* taught me about finding my true calling, and *The Wizard of Oz* helped me see the power God had already given me. Each story was like a mirror showing me different parts of my own spiritual growth. They taught me that when we see clearly, follow God's path, and use the gifts He gave us, we can become who He meant for us to be.

As you think about your own life, know this: like Cinderella, you have gifts from God waiting for you; like the teacher, you have something special only you can do; and like Dorothy, you already have everything you need to become who God created you to be.

ABOUT THE AUTHOR

Dr. Veronica Deas is a passionate educator, speaker, and faith leader whose life mission is simple yet profound: *"Know who you are and Whose you are."* With over 30 years of teaching experience, she has inspired thousands through her work in education, as well as her leadership with the *Value of a Woman* organization, where she spearheads conferences and hosts a dynamic podcast.

Dr. Deas holds a B.A. in Accounting, an MBA, and an Ed.D. in Educational and Organizational Leadership—credentials that reflect both her intellectual rigor and her commitment to equipping others for growth. Blending her love for studying God's Word, teaching, fashion, and storytelling, she brings a unique voice to the intersection of faith and practical living.

A resident of Goose Creek, South Carolina, Dr. Deas now turns her decades of wisdom toward empowering readers through her literary publications.

www.ingramcontent.com/pod-product-compliance
Lightning Source LLC
Chambersburg PA
CBHW072137070526
44585CB00016B/1717